2/97

Myths and Legends of
CREATION
OF THE WORLD

Claude-Catherine Ragache
Illustrated by Marcel Lavardat

MARSHALL CAVENDISH
New York · London · Toronto · Sydney

Library Edition Published 1991

Published by Marshall Cavendish Corporation
2415 Jerusalem Avenue
PO Box 587, North Bellmore,
N.Y. 11710
Library edition produced by Pemberton Press
Printed by Colorcraft Ltd. in Hong Kong

Ⓒ Marshall Cavendish Corporation 1991
Ⓒ Cherrytree Press Ltd. 1990

Adapted by AS Publishing from La Chevalerie, published by Hachette.

Library of Congress Cataloging-in-Publication Data

Ragache, Claude-Catherine.

     Creation of the world / Claude-Catherine Ragache: edited by
Gilles Ragache; translated by Abigail Frost; illustrations by
Marcel Lavardat.
     p. cm. – (Myths & Legends)
    Includes Index.
    Summary: Explores the numerous myths and legends attempting to
explain the creation of the world.
    ISBN 1-85435-264-4;
    1. Creation – Juvenile literature. 2. Mythology – Juvenile
literature. (1. Creation. 2 Mythology.) I. Ragache. Gilles.
II. Lavardat, Marcel, III. III. Title, IV. Series: Frost, Abigail.
Myths and Legends.
BL325.C7R34 1991
291.2`4 – dc20
                            80-25283
                              CIP
                              AC

CONTENTS

▷ YMIR, THE ICE GIANT ◁

When time began, nothing existed but a bottomless abyss of empty space. This was bounded to the north by a frozen land from which flowed twelve streams of ice. To the south lay a land of fire; rivers of boiling, steaming water gushed from it, but as they flowed northward they too froze over. And so little by little the gulf of space was filled by ice.

Then a warm wind from the south began to blow across the desolate icecap. A drop of water formed on its surface; this was soon followed by many more, which flowed together and formed themselves into a giant, called Ymir. The warm wind made him perspire, and the drops of sweat that ran from him turned into more giants. Meanwhile, water from the melting ice turned into the cow Audhumla who gave milk to feed the giants.

As the giants milked Audhumla, she licked the blocks of ice around her. Under her warm rough tongue there appeared first hair, then a head, and finally a whole body; that of another living being, Buri.

Buri was the father of the first three gods of the Scandinavian world; Olin, Vili, and Ve. Before long, a terrible war broke out between the giants and the gods, and almost all the giants were killed. Only one giant and one giantess managed to escape to the farthest lands of the north.

The gods looked about them at their dreary, frozen kingdom. They decided to create a new world – but what could they make it from? Their glance fell on the frozen, lifeless body of the giant Ymir. Together, they heaved it into space and transformed it into the Earth; they called it Midgard. They took Ymir's skull and placed in on four tall pillars to make the vault of the sky. They turned sparks from the land of fire into stars with which to decorate it, and set it with a burning coal which formed the Sun and gave their new world light.

Next, the gods built themselves a marvelous palace in the sky. It was as big as a city. The family of gods grew, and they often gathered together in the palace and held great feasts there. From time to time they would cross over a rainbow bridge to walk around the Earth. For a long time the only living beings there were dwarfs, who lived in caves deep underground and forged the metals they found there.

One day, three gods who were strolling along a beach came across two dead trees. "Let's bring them back to life!" they said. Odin breathed life into the trees; Hoener gave them spirit and sense; and Lodur gave them warmth and color.

The trees stirred, changed shape, and drew breath – the gods had formed them into the first man and the first woman.

As the ice melted, drops of water flowed together to form the giant Ymir.

THE EAGLE WITH THE GOLDEN EGGS

For hundreds of years, Luonnotar, the beautiful daughter of Nature, glided through the empty blue sky, until at last she grew tired of her lonely existence. Far below stretched a boundless sea. Luonnotar gathered all her strength and dived down, down into the water. Then she stretched out on its calm surface.

Soon a violent wind sprang up, and for a long time Luonnotar was tossed like a little boat on the angry waves. When calm returned at last, she knew that she was going to have a son; but he could only be born when she had prepared a world for him to live in.

For nine long years, Luonnotar searched the limitless sea in vain for a shore where she could stop and rest. At last, cold and miserable, she prayed for pity to the great god Ukko, lord of the vast regions of the air. Blinded by her tears, she did not see an eagle soaring above her. It was a female, looking for somewhere to build her nest. But the world of wind and water provided no perch, and she began to fly away. Luonnotar heard her desolate cries and, stretching on her back to see the bird, she lifted one knee above the waves. The eagle dropped straight on this islet which had appeared so providentially, and there she laid seven eggs: the first six were gold, and the seventh was made of iron.

For three days the eagle sat on her eggs. Luonnotar dared not move, but by the end of the third day she could stay still no longer. She straightened out her leg and shook it. The eggs rolled into the sea and smashed. Then, under Luonnotar's astonished gaze, the largest piece of golden eggshell floated upward and grew and grew to form the vault of the sky. The other pieces turned into the Earth; the yolks became the Sun and the whites the Moon. The tiniest fragments of eggshell became the stars and the clouds.

For nine years more Luonnotar explored her new world. But it was flat and featureless, and she grew bored by it. She decided to reshape it. She built mountains and islands and carved out valleys. She dived into the ocean to form its caverns and gulfs, and when she returned to land the water streaming from her body became rivers and lakes. At last she was satisfied. She gave birth to her son, the hero Waïnämöinen, who tilled and cultivated the Earth his mother had made for him.

Luonnotar reshaped Earth to make it fit for her son to live in.

THE SONS OF EARTH AND SKY

Before the Earth was formed, there was nothing; no form, no movements, no sounds, no scents, no light, no life, no matter. There was only limitless emptiness. And no one can say how long this lasted, for time itself did not exist.

At last a faint scent stole through this nothingness and gradually grew stronger. It came from the direction which people, much later, would call the east. Then – still from the east – came the first dim rays of light. And in the rays of light danced specks of dust – for movement and matter were born together. The great upheaval which would lead to the formation of the Universe had begun.

Little by little two beings grew up in this cosmic chaos. These were the Earth, Papa, and the Sky, Rangi. At first Papa and Rangi floated through space, far from each other. But an irresistible force drew them together until they were tightly entwined. Soon they gave birth to the gods.

The gods grew strong and powerful, but they were trapped in the darkness between their parents. Only Tawhire, god of the winds, was able to slide between them and move freely. The others decided they must do something about this. Tu, the most violent, wanted to kill Papa and Rangi. His brothers agreed that they must try to separate Sky and Earth – but gently, without hurting them. Tane, the god of the forests, was put in charge of the operation. He placed his head on his mother Papa, the Earth, and with his feet against the Sky he pushed and pushed until at last he had separated his parents. At once the world was filled with light.

The Sky was furious to be separated from his wife Papa; he summoned Tawhire, god of the winds, and ordered him to let loose a tempest on the Earth where his brothers were living. Tawhire produced a hurricane which uprooted the trees of the forests and whipped up the waves of the sea into a frenzy. All the land was flooded. But still Tane kept pushing his parents apart.

Now came a fearful struggle. Although most of the gods hid underground, Tu fought on Tane's side, and in the end he was victorious. The storm died down and the floods subsided. Tawhire was banished to exile near his father, the Sky. Tu gave each of his other brothers their own kingdom, but he was to be their overlord.

Now he was master of the world. He took a handful of red clay, and from it he created the first woman, Hine, to live there with him and be his wife. Their sons and daughters were the first people.

Bracing himself against the Earth, Tane forced his parents Earth and Sky apart.

SEA CRYSTALS

When the Universe was still in chaos, the gods asked the genies Izanagi and Izanami to create the world. What a task! All that existed was a vast, thick, and oily ocean beneath an empty sky.

Izanagi and Izanami wondered where to begin. They flew over the ocean on a heavenly raft, but they could find nothing which looked like land. "If land exists, its heavy particles would sink to the very bottom of the Universe," they decided. So they fetched a long lance of jade, encrusted with a thousand jewels and shining with a thousand fires.

When the tip of the lance touched the surface of the ocean, Izanagi and Izanami began to stir it as if they were stirring a stewpot. The thick liquid grew thicker still until crystals began to form in it. The genies lifted up their lance and shook it; the drops which fell from it turned into an island called Onogoro.

"Let's go down and live on that island," suggested Izanagi. "We can marry, and continue our task from there." So the two genies traveled down a rainbow to their new home.

Before they married, Izanagi and Izanami walked around Onogoro, to show that they owned it. Izanagi went clockwise and Izanami went counterclockwise. When they met again, Izanami cried; "How happy I am that we are to be married, Izanagi." "Foolish one," he replied. "You should not have spoken first, since you are a woman. We must begin the ceremony again."

This time all went well. But because of Izanami's mistake before their marriage, the first islands were misshapen, so they gave them back to the ocean. The next were perfect, and they became the eight main islands of Japan.

Izanagi and Izanami leaned from their raft to stir the ocean with their lance of jade.

ENA AND ATA

Long, long ago when the world was nothing but a vast ocean, three gods reigned in the Sky: Tagaola the Noble; Tagaola the Workman; and Tagaola the Silent, who saw things before they even existed.

All three were curious to know if there were lands under the ocean, and Tagaola the Silent was asked by his companions to go down from the sky to find out. He took the form of a kingfisher and flew over the tips of the waves. There was no sign of land. At last he saw a pale patch under the water's surface. Did this mean that land might appear there? It was too soon to tell.

When seven days had passed, the kingfisher set out again. Now he could see a rock just below the surface. So Tagaola the Workman threw down stones from the Sky, which piled up on the rock and formed Ena, the very first island in the world.

After the gods had made this first land, Tagaola the Silent made many flights to the pale patch, where little by little fine sand appeared above the waves until it formed Ata, Mother Earth.

"This land is splendid, but there are no trees on it!" said the explorer to the other gods. So Tagaola the Noble gave him a seed to sow, and soon the island was covered with a creeping plant.

"This land is splendid, but there are no people on it," said Tagaola the Silent.

"Go and cut a piece of creeper," replied Tagaola the Noble. And the little piece of creeper he cut was transformed into the very first two human beings.

Stones hurled down by the gods from heaven built up the island of Ena.

11

NUM AND THE MAN FROM NOWHERE

Over the primordial ocean hovered the great god Num. "The land is hidden deep, deep in the ocean," he said to himself as he surveyed the deserted waters. "I must raise it to the surface so that I can create Earth. Who can find it for me?" He thought of the birds, the only living creatures in the early days of the Universe.

"Dive down and find the land," he ordered the swans and geese. They disappeared into the ocean, but surfaced again soon afterward having found nothing. Next Num gave the same mission to a diving duck. For six days Num waited; and when at last the bird surfaced it explained: "I have found the land, but my strength gave out; I could not raise it." So Num sent down an Arctic bird named Ljuru. Seven days later he reappeared, carrying in his beak a small piece of mud.

Now Num began to build an island. It grew larger each day. One evening, he looked up to see beside him a cross old man leaning on a stick. "Where did you come from?" asked Num. "Oh, from somewhere around . . . " replied the old man, "I'm tired; let me rest here."

"Out of the question," snapped Num. "Only those who take part in building it have the right to set foot on Earth."

The old man was so insistent that Num finally gave in. The next morning the god saw the old man crouching down beside the water. "He's not so bad after all," thought Num; "he understood that he should help, and has set to work." But when he drew closer Num found that the old man was pulling the island to pieces.

"So this is how you thank me! Go away at once!" thundered Num.

"Calm down!" said the old man. "I'll go and you need never see me again – but on one condition: give me a little piece of land, as big as I can cover with the point of my stick."

Num was happy to think that he would be rid of the horrid old man so easily and readily agreed to give him the land. But before Num could stop him, the old man dug out a hole into which he disappeared, saying triumphantly: "You reign on Earth, Num, but I will set up my kingdom under it. You will create living beings; but at the end of their life, I shall draw them into my kingdom through this hole."

Num understood now that the old man was the lord of the Underworld, who had taken a little of his power from him forever.

The old man was destroying the newly built Earth . . .

13

THE GIANT'S CHALLENGE

When the world began, the Earth and the Sky together formed one solid mass. A giant named Khong-Lo, whose height was immense and whose strength was enormous, undertook to separate them. He began by straddling the sky and heaving it up onto his shoulders; the huge mass broke up with a thundering crack. The effort was so great that the giant blew out his breath in an enormous tempest.

When he straightened himself up again, Khong-Lo molded the Sky into the shape of an upturned bowl. He dug huge blocks of stone out of the flat surface of the Earth, and used them to build a pillar to hold the vault of the sky in place while it dried and set. Once this had happened, the giant pulled down the pillar, scattering the stones around him. The ground shook under the weight of the rocks which bounced in a cloud of dust before settling on the Earth to form its first mountains. Other stones rolled into the craters dug out by the giant, which had filled with water; these formed the Earth's first islands.

Hardly had Khong-Lo finished his work when an even larger giant appeared beside him. This was a woman, and immediately Khong-Lo asked her to marry him. She did not refuse him, but instead she challenged him to prove what sort of a giant he might be. "Let each of us build a mountain in three days. If yours is higher than mine you will be the winner, and then I will marry you."

Khong-Lo, his heart full of hope, piled up the most enormous rocks that he could find. But when the three days were passed, the huge mountain he had built was completely over-shadowed by the vast mountain built by the giantess. To make matters worse, not content with winning she kicked over Khong-Lo's mountain contemptuously with her toe.

"I will give you another chance," she said. "See this river; you must dam it in a single night." Despite his strength, the giant was good tempered and showed that he bore no resentment. He set to work cheerfully, and soon felt sure of victory. Only a trickle of the river still ran down the riverbed, and dawn was still far away. But at that moment, he heard a rooster crow. "What! Daybreak already? I must have made a mistake," he said to himself, stopping work at once. But the Sky grew no lighter, and before very long he angrily realized that he had been tricked. The giantess herself had crowed like a rooster to halt him when she saw that he was winning!

Despite her nasty ways – and only after he had carried out many more tasks which she gave him – Khong-Lo eventually married the mischievous giantess; but it seems unlikely that they lived happily ever after!

14

Good-tempered Khong-Lo accepted challenges from the cheating giantess

The Universe is made up of the sky, the Earth, the Sun, the stars, the Moon, and the planets. Since earliest times, people have thought up all kinds of stories to explain how the Universe began. They have also tried to picture what shape the Universe might be, and many have come up with some fascinating ideas.

Of course even today, despite all the advances in our knowledge, and all our modern scientific instruments, we still do now know just how the Universe began, nor its shape or size!

The cosmic egg

An ancient Chinese tradition shows the Universe as an egg standing on its end. The lower half is filled with the primordial ocean, in which the Earth floats like the yolk; the inside surface of the upper part of the eggshell forms the sky. At the center of the egg lived the giant Pan-Ku. Each day for eighteen thousand years he grew by several feet. Before long his head was pressing against the sky; the eggshell broke and his head pushed the sky farther and farther above the Earth until the day he died. Then his head became a sacred mountain, and his eyes turned into the Sun and the Moon. His hair was transformed into the trees.

A Hindu myth tells that the Universe came from an egg made of gold and silver. The sky came from a piece of golden eggshell, and the Earth from a fragment of silver shell.

Holding up the sky

How is the sky held in place over the Earth? Simple: it rests on pillars, said a Chinese myth. This story represented the Earth as flat and square, with a column supporting the sky at each corner. The sky was circular and rotated around the Pole Star, taking with it all the stars which were fixed to its surface.

But this arrangement was nearly destroyed by the monster Kong-Kong; furious at not being master of the Universe, he threw himself violently against the northwest column so that it became dangerously shaky. As a result, the sky sags in that direction. The Sun and stars are displaced towards the northwest while the Earth is tilted to the northeast. This is the reason, the myth explains, why all the great rivers of China run in that direction.

Shaping the Earth's surface

Many civilizations thought that the Earth had a flat surface when it was first created. Mountains were formed later, perhaps when angry gods or powerful giants shook

One world above another

Other myths, from regions as far apart as America, Scandinavia, and Oceania, describe the Universe as a collection of worlds one above another, held in place by a central pole or by a giant tree.

According to an ancient Scandinavian legend the oak tree Yggdrasil supported the Universe. Its roots were in the frozen underground world of the giants; its topmost branches reached the sky where the gods lived. Among its branches were many animals, including a cock, an eagle, and a squirrel, while its roots were nibbled away by a monster that was half dragon, half serpent. But thanks to a miraculous spring from which one of its roots fed, the oak was able to survive. Halfway up Yggdrasil was Earth, surrounded by a vast ocean. In this swam an immense reptile, whose coils held together the lands in which people lived.

The islanders of Nauru in Micronesia told how the god Solal stuck a pole into a rock floating in a primordial ocean. Then Solal climbed up the pole, pausing halfway up to create the Earth before he went on to the top of the pole where he set up the Sky.

the ground. The people of Madagascar tell how the Sky and Earth, which were male and female, often argued fiercely with each other. During their quarrels the Sky threw down torrents of rain and avalanches of stones. In return the Earth sent up spurts of flaming lava from its volcanoes. Peace came only when the gods managed to calm the opponents; but scars from their battles are still visible on the Earth's surface in the form of hills and lake beds.

Earth movements

Other myths explain events such as earthquakes. According to people living in Siberia, an old man living in Hell holds the Earth in his hand. But he gets tired and trembles, and then the whole Earth shakes.

An Arab myth describes how the Earth is held up by an enormous whale. To prevent it from moving and shaking the Earth, God made a tiny creature which watches it carefully, threatening to creep into its nostril if it makes the slightest movement.

▷ YI AND THE TEN SUNS ◁

Every morning, one of the ten suns rose to the tip of the giant mulberry tree in which he and his brothers spent the night. While his brothers rested in the lower branches, he took his place in a flaming chariot drawn by six dragons, and sped toward the sky. Once every ten days it was his turn to bring light and warmth to the world and everything that lived on it. For the next nine days he rested in the mulberry tree and built up his strength.

Everyone was happy with this arrangement. "If one of the suns has an accident, we have nine more in reserve! All ten suns will never go out at the same time!" they said. And they added: "One sun in the sky, one emperor on Earth, that is all we need."

Then, early one morning, the peasants working in the fields were surprised to find that the day was already exceedingly hot. Soon they could no longer stay bent over their paddy fields; their large hats could not shield them from the glare reflected from the water, and their backs burned in the intense heat of not one but of all ten suns! Before long the paddy fields had dried out and the young shoots of rice had shriveled. Fires began to break out. Everything on Earth was in danger; but how could the suns' mad race be stopped?

Yi the Fowler raised the Emperor's magic bow.

Yao, Emperor of China, was as powerful as a god. He possessed a magic bow which could shoot arrows so far that they were lost in space. "We must kill nine of the ten suns with my magic bow," he said. Was there an archer skilled enough to hit such distant targets?

Yi the Fowler was famous for his strength and his skill; his arrows never missed their mark. The Emperor gave him the magic bow. By now it was noon; the suns were at the highest point of their journey and their rays were at their most powerful. There was not an instant to lose. Yi knelt down, drew his bow, and aimed at one of the murderous suns. The arrow sped from the bow so quickly that no one could see it. Yi watched anxiously until he saw that the sun dwindled and grew dark. Eight times he repeated his draw; and eight times a sun died. When there was only one sun left, everyone ran from the shade where they had been hiding and called out joyfully "Yi has saved the Earth!"

From then on, Yi was revered as a god. He traveled all over the world, and one day he reached the western edge of the world where the sun went down. There, on a jade mountain, lived the Mother Queen of the West. To reward Yi, she gave him some of the elixir of immortal life. But when Yi returned home, his wife stole the precious drink from him and, changing herself into a toad, fled to the Moon. Even now, you can sometimes see her shadow on the Moon's surface.

CENTRAL AMERICA

▷ THE FIFTH WORLD ◁

Long, long ago, Tezcatlipoca, the god of the North, of cold, and of rain ruled over the world. It was different from our world; it was the first world of all. One day Tezcatlipoca turned himself into a huge and powerful jaguar; he sprang up into the Sky and gulped down the Sun! And so the first world came to an end.

A second world came into being; and this one was brought to an end by the god Quetzalcoatl. While magicians turned all the people into monkeys, he called up westerly winds so violent that they destroyed everything in their path.

The third world was destroyed by molten lava from the sky, sent by Tlaloc, the god of thunder, lightning, and volcanoes; and the fourth world was flooded by a downpour sent by the goddess of water, which lasted for 52 years until the skies fell in. Just one man and one woman managed to take refuge at the tip of a cypress tree. But, in the end, Tlaloc found them and turned them into dogs. When the waters finally subsided, there was no human life left on Earth.

Now a fifth world had to be created, for this was the Law of the Universe. First, Quetzalcoatl went down to the Lower Kingdom where the dead lived; he restored them to life once more. Then the gods lifted back the Sky, and created the Sun and Moon to lighten the darkness with which the Earth was shrouded.

"Which of us shall give light to the world?" they asked one another.

"I shall do it," answered Tecciztecatl, an impressive and splendidly clothed god.

"Anyone else?"

"I would like to, as well," said a quiet little voice. The gods turned to the speaker, and were astonished to see the small and shabby god Nanauatzin. But they accepted his offer with relief, for it would be a fearful ordeal to become the Sun or the Moon.

The gods lit a huge fire, and the two volunteers made offerings. Tecciztecatl gave gold rings, jewels, and priceless feathers. All Nanauatzin could offer were some reeds, some wisps of hay, and some thorns which scratched his hands. They were given new garments; a cloak of feathers and fine cloth for Tecciztecatl, and a cap and shirt of paper for Nanauatzin. Then they climbed to the top of two pyramids from which they must hurl themselves into the fire – for only then could they be reborn as Sun or Moon.

Four times Tecciztecatl stepped to the brink of the pyramid, but each time he was too afraid to jump. Little Nanauatzin sprang without hesitating into the flames; and emerged from them as the Sun. This encouraged Tecciztecatl and he too jumped into the fire, to emerge as the Moon.

"Where shall the Sun and Moon rise?" asked the gods. In the end, the Sun and Moon decided to rise in the east. First came the Sun, so bright and splendid that no one could look directly at it; what a transformation for shabby, timid Nanauatzin. The Moon – the former Tecciztecatl – came out almost at the same time, and was just as splendid. But this did not please some of the gods.

"They should not both light up the Earth in the same way," they said to one another. So they threw a hare at the Moon, which dimmed its brilliance and left its paw marks on the surface; and you can see them to this day.

The gods Nanauatzin and Tecciztecatl, transformed into Sun and Moon, rose together.

SIBERIA
THE HEAVENLY REINDEER

The first reindeer had six legs so that they could escape hunters more easily. Just as they were about to be caught, they would stamp on the ground, give a great bound, and disappear into the distance.

One day a huge reindeer roamed up to a hunters' camp, frightening their animals' which ran away in panic. The most skillful of the hunters set out after it. His skis skimmed over the snow at the speed of light. Little by little he gained on the reindeer until he had almost caught up, but just as he was ready to throw a rope over the reindeer's head it gave a mighty bound into the Sky. At the same moment the hunter's skis grew light, and he realized that he too was speeding through the air, close behind the reindeer.

But the hunter never quite caught up. We can still see the two of them today among the stars; the reindeer has become the Pole Star, and the hunter the constellation known as the Pleiades, while the tracks of his skis form the Milky Way.

FINLAND
THE GIANT OAK

Long ago, when the world was still young, three young girls planted an oak tree. All three were soon to be married, and perhaps they thought this tree would bring them luck.

Years passed, and the tree grew and grew until it was one of the most splendid in the region. Although the girls who had planted it were long forgotten, people came from far and wide to admire their tree. But when they saw that, huge as it was, it was still steadily growing, they began to wonder.

One day, a little cloud was puffed by the wind into the topmost branches of the tree, and was trapped there; the treetop had reached the Sky. Then a series of disasters followed. More and more clouds became entangled in the branches, which grew too densely for them to avoid; the weather became worse and worse. Finally even the Sun and Moon found their paths blocked. They came to a halt, and all the trapped clouds surrounding them stopped their light from shining down on Earth. The whole world became dark and cold, and people were in despair.

Try as they might, no one could cut down the huge oak. All seemed hopeless. Then a tiny man swam to the surface of the sea. He was only as tall as three thumbs, and his hair and his skin were dark. In his hand he carried a tiny hatchet made of solid gold. He stepped up to the immense tree, beside which he looked almost invisible, and with a single stroke of his hatchet he severed the vast trunk.

The watchers held their breath; where would the tree fall – and what harm would it do? But instead of crashing to the ground, the great trunk whirled up, up into the Sky. All the clouds trapped in the tree's branches wiggled themselves free and blew away. The Sun and Moon took up their journeys again, and their light shone down and warmed the Earth once more. Life could get back to normal. But some stars were still caught in the branches of the giant tree, which now floated far away in the heavens; they became the Milky Way.

The trunk of the great oak whirled up into the heavens . . .

MYTHS ABOUT THE SKY AND STARS

The sky is the most mysterious part of the Universe. It is a source of help and harm; from the sky come both gentle rain to help us grow our food, and fierce, destructive storms. Not surprisingly, people both feared and respected it and thought of it as the home of the gods. Above all, the sky has been looked on as the home of the Sun and the Moon, sacred in many civilizations, and of the stars.

The Sun

Egyptians, Japanese, Incas and many other people worshiped the Sun, the bringer of light and warmth. But the Sun could also provide a destructive enemy. The ancient Japanese told how tears from the right eye of the genie Izanagi gave birth to the Sun, while those from the left eye gave birth to the Moon. According to Hindu legend, the eye of the giant Purusha was transformed into the Sun.

The Polynesian hero Maui dared to change the course of the Sun, which was rising so late in the morning and setting so early in the afternoon that people did not have enough time to carry out their daily work during the hours of daylight. Maui made a long rope from his own hair and formed a running noose at its end. Then he lay in wait for the Sun.

Just as it rose over the horizon, he lassoed it with his rope, and hung onto it for all he was worth. He could not stop the Sun, but he managed to slow down its journey.

Each night the Sun disappears. "Will it rise again?"

worried the Pygmies. Fortunately, one of their gods sprinkled it with a handful of stars each morning, which revived its flames.

The Moon

Many legends tell how two Suns were born at the same time, which gave too much light and heat. Some say that the Suns were jealous of each other; according to an African legend the first Sun suggested to the second that they should bathe, but only pretended to jump into the water. The second sun dashed into the river, and its light was almost washed away; it became the Moon.

was lifted a fraction and then the heroes could squeeze through the gap to rejoin the gods living above the clouds.

The nomads of the Urals imagine the sky as a tent with one flap unfastened; its movements cause the wind. They also think that the sky becomes much lower as it nears the horizon; people and animals become smaller and smaller as they reach this region, and there is only one passage through, for migrant birds.

The rainbow

When the gods wish to communicate with human beings, the call up a rainbow. Scandinavian and Japanese legends tell how they use it as a bridge to cross from the sky to the Earth. But evil creatures can also use this path, and the god Heimdall keeps a constant watch at the foot of the rainbow Bifrost, to prevent giants from crossing it to attack the kingdom of the gods.

The stars

One night a North American coyote was ordered to arrange the stars in their correct order. As he hurried over his task he tripped, and the stars spilled out and scattered all over the sky. The Pole Star, which guides travelers, marks the opening through which dead Indians and heroes pass from the Earth to the sky. Some nomadic tribes of central Asia think that the Pole Star is the stake to which the rest of the stars are tied.

Covering the Earth

According to the Chinese, the sky is held in place over the Earth by four giant columns. The ancient Greeks tell how the giant Atlas, punished for fighting the god Zeus, carries the sky on his shoulders. The Iroquois of North America thought of the sky as the lid of an immense cauldron containing boiling water; sometimes the lid

THE GIRL WHO FELL FROM THE SKY

Long ago, before people came to Earth, they lived in another world; it was just like ours, but it lay beyond the Sky.

One day a young girl called Ataensic, who lived in this distant world, was weeding in the fields near her home. Her dog lay beside her. Suddenly she heard grunts and snarls in a nearby thicket, and before she could stop him her little dog dashed into it.

Next came furious barking, and then an enormous bear lumbered out with the dog snapping at its heels!

Ataensic was terrified, but she followed their tracks until she came on them at the edge of a precipice. She saw her dog spring for the bear's throat, and together they fell from sight. With a cry of horror Ataensic ran to the edge of the precipice, hoping against hope that her dog might have landed on some branch or rock. But when she leaned over the edge she could see nothing at all – not even the bottom of the cliff. She leaned a little farther and, losing her balance, toppled over the edge. Down, down she fell – for Ataensic had slipped into an open crack in the vault of the Sky.

Far below the world from which she fell stretched a vast ocean. No rock or island broke its surface, and no shores fringed its edges; but it was not lifeless, for in it lived the turtle, the beaver, the muskrat, and many other water animals. The first to notice Ataensic was the turtle. "Come quickly and see what is falling from the Sky," he called to the other animals. "It looks like a living creature!"

Birds flew up to bring Ataensic gently to Earth.

The animals felt sure that the new arrival would not be able to swim. How could they stop her drowning? "Quick," ordered the wise turtle. "We must build a surface on which the creature can land. Dive down to the bottom of the sea and bring up as much mud as you can." The beaver spreak the mud over the turtle's shell with his flat tail and shaped it into an island. Meanwhile the sea birds flew to meet Ataensic and guided her gently down. The island the animals built was the first land on Earth. Later it grew so large that it covered much of the ocean, and Ataensic and her descendants were the ancestors of the North American Indians.

CENTRAL AMERICA

▷ THE FOUR CREATIONS ◁

When the world was very new – so new that only the Sky and the sea existed – seven gods held a council. There were the gods of the North, South, East and West; Tepeu the Workman; Gucumatz the Ruler, with his cloak of green feathers, and Huracan Skyheart.

When they had all settled down, Huracan called up a great flash of lightning and a growling roll of thunder. "Earth!" he cried; and as he spoke the sea seethed and bubbled, and land formed above its surface, complete with mountains and valleys and covered with lush green vegetation. Gucumatz was delighted.

"What is the point of the Earth if there is no one to enjoy it?" asked another of the gods. "Let's create some perfect beings to live there,

who will worship us and sing our praises."

So the gods settled down to their new task. First they created birds, snakes, and wild animals. "Now worship us and sing our praises," they commanded. But the animals had no voices; they could only whistle, grunt, or bark. The disappointed gods realized that their first creations were far from perfect, "From now on, you will be hunted, killed, and eaten," they said crossly.

The gods decided to try again. They took some damp earth and shaped it into human beings. But again they made a mistake; although these beings could talk, when the earth dried they were so solid that they could not turn their heads, but looked straight in front –

and what was more serious, they dissolved if they got wet! Worst of all, the gods had given them no intelligence. Angrily, they destroyed their creations and thought again. "Let's try wood," they said.

Soon Earth was filled with wooden people. They talked, they had children, they built houses – but they had no feelings. They never thought about their creators. The disappointed gods drove them from the Earth. Only a very few managed to hide themselves in the forests, where they gave birth to little tree-dwelling monkeys.

The gods were determined to create their perfect people, cost what it might. They called another council. "We must find a truly noble substance with which to form the flesh and blood of these people – something which will also give them life, strength and intelligence," they said. "But where can we find such a thing?"

As they pondered, four animals came to find them; the wildcat, the coyote, the parakeet, and the kite. "We know where you can find just what you want," they said "Follow us!"

They led the gods to a field where yellow and white corn was growing.

"Here are the magic plants from which we can make our people!" exclaimed the gods. They plucked the corncobs, ground the white and yellow grains to flour, and made a paste from which they formed four people. At last they had succeeded. These people thanked their creators and sang their praises. They became as intelligent as the gods themselves, and they could even see in the dark. The gods were uneasy. "We have done our work too well," they said to one another. "We must check their powers." So the gods threw mist over the eyes of the people, which dimmed their sight until they could only see things close to them. Then the gods were satisfied at last.

The gods' early efforts to create people were not a success.

▷ QAT'S DANCE ◁

Long, long ago Earth was an arid desert burning under a constant Sun; no tides stirred the seas, and no clouds sailed across the Sky. All was silent and still. Then suddenly a huge, solitary rock exploded and out sprang the god Qat the Creator. Immediately he set to work. First he created plants, and great trees soon shaded the world and made it fit to live in. Next Qat created animals, starting with the pig, and then he set out to make human beings.

Qat took a branch from one of his trees and carefully carved the bodies of three men and three women from it. Then he placed them in the shade and left them there to season. When the figures were ready, Qat came back and danced around them, beating a drum. Slowly the figures began to breathe and then to move; Qat was bringing them to life!

Qat was so enthralled by his work that he did not notice his jealous brother Marawa watching from a thicket. "I've seen just what Qat has done, and now it's my turn to do the same," Marawa decided. And so he did; but when his figures began to move, he hid them in a hollow in the forest. Alas, he left them there too long and they died; and since then, humans have been mortal.

▷ MULUKU AND THE MONKEY MEN ◁

The great god Muluku dug two holes in the Earth, and pulled out two living creatures. They stood upright on their back legs, and looked at him as if waiting for orders.

"Here are Man and Woman!" cried Muluku happily. He thought that he had given life to intelligent creatures, and he decided to give them a test. "Listen carefully," he said. "Here is a pick; till the soil with it, then sow some millet from this bag. With the ax, cut down branches and build a shelter. When you are hungry, cook some millet in this pot. I will leave you burning logs for a fire; don't let it die out!" And Muluku, who had other things to attend to, soared away from Earth.

Some time later, Muluku came back to see how his people were getting on. But where was the hut he had told them to build? The cooking pot lay broken beside the ashes of the fire, and nearby lay the empty millet bag and the pick. At last Muluku found the people in the forest; they had decided not to work, but to live like the animals.

Muluku flew into a rage. Calling two apes, he gave them the same tools and the same orders. The two animals did just as he had asked. So Muluku said to them: "From now on, you shall be human beings!" Then he seized the man and the woman, and said sternly: "Now you are monkeys; that is all you are worth."

TIBET

THE MONKEY AND THE ROCK DEMON

A very long time ago a monkey was climbing the slopes of an enormous mountain. At last he reached the land of snow at the roof of the world, where only demons lived. In front of him yawned an ice cavern which reflected the Sun in a thousand points of light. The monkey sat down in prayer in front of it. He was in fact a follower of Buddha, who had taken the shape of a monkey to prepare the land of snows for the arrival of human beings.

The monkey sat motionless in the deep silence, unconscious of cold and hunger. Suddenly he was startled by a fearful shriek. He looked up to see a terrifying demon jumping about in front of him, waving its arms, making hideous faces, and screaming.

"Go away and leave me in peace," begged the monkey. The demon disappeared, only to reappear at once behind him. "Marry me," she cried. "I have fallen in love with you. If you will not, I will marry another demon and produce a multitude of little demons, who will eat a thousand living creatures every day!" What was the monkey to do?

For seven days running the demon appeared. At last the monkey asked Buddha's advice, and much to his surprise he was told to marry her!

Soon the demon bore him six sons. They inherited their father's red face and furry body. All of them could talk, but only the eldest was kind and generous. The others were mean and jealous, stupid and violent. The monkey led his children down the mountain to the shelter of a forest where real monkeys lived, and then went back to pray in his icy cavern.

After a few months the monkey went to see how his children were getting on. To his surprise he found not six of them, but five hundred! They had changed to look more like humans. Some were civilized, but others were still savage and violent. All of them suffered terribly from cold in winter and heat in summer, from the rain and the wind; and all of them were hungry. The monkey took pity of his children and said to Buddha: "I did as you wanted, but see how miserable my poor children are. Do not leave them like this."

"Be patient," Buddha replied. "Little by little your children are changing into people; soon their monkey tails will fall off, and they will leave the forest to live in more pleasant places. I will help them. Here are three strands of wool, a handful of barley, and some fragments of precious metal. I have taken them from the treasure hidden at the heart of the sacred mountain in the center of the world; they will decide the fate of your children."

Buddha put these objects down on the snow. Some of the monkey's children settled where he had put the strands of wool and became shepherds. Some settled where the grains of barley had fallen and became farmers. The other settled where the pieces of precious metal were laid and became metalworkers. So the children of the monkey and the demon of the rocks became the first people to live in the land of snow at the roof of the world, which we know as Tibet.

The monkey's children became the first people of Tibet.

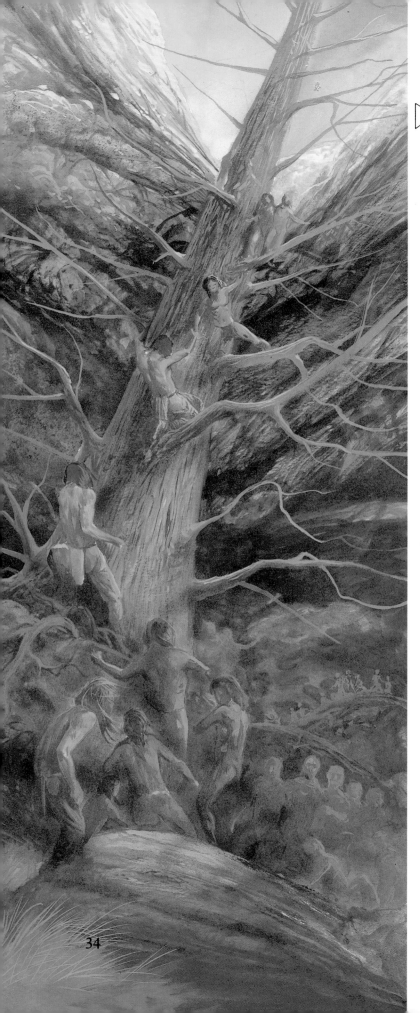

MYTHS ABOUT PEOPLE

How did human beings appear on Earth? Did they come down from another world, by accident or as a punishment, or were they created by the gods specially to live on Earth? And why are they not all the same?

People from other places . . .

According to legends told by the North American Indians, the first people came from a dark underground world where they lived on all fours like animals. They reached the Earth's surface by climbing a giant pine tree. Then, helped by a god (in some versions of the legend, they were helped by the goddess of maize) they learned to cultivate the soil.

The Eskimos believed that the pillars which had once held up the sky crumbled, overturning the Earth and making its first inhabitants the spirits of the underworld. Later two hillocks appeared on the Earth's surface, from which emerged a new people, the Eskimos. In the early days, they said, Eskimo women who were not married were able to find children – particularly girls – in the ground.

The Indians thought that people had once lived on another world, far above the sky; then one of them fell through a hole in the sky and they came to colonize our planet.

Creator gods

According to most mythologies, human beings were created by the gods. Some stories tell how they shaped them out of raw materials such as clay or sand or wood. Sometimes the gods made their first people out of plants valued for their nourishing qualities, such as maize (the Maya), or coconut or sugarcane (Polynesians). The people of the New Hebrides tell how the first man was made of clay, and the first woman out of palm fronds. But the gods often made mistakes, and succeeded in creating people only after several attempts.

Why people are different

A tribe living in the White Nile region thought the god Juok created all the people on Earth. He used pale sand to create fair-skinned races, and the tawny sand of Egypt for the brown-skinned Mediterranean and Arab peoples. The Negroes of Africa were made from the dark earth of their region. Another African myth tells how black-skinned people were made in the strong light of day, while people with paler skin were made in moonlight.

In Indochina the first people flew like birds and could talk to plants and animals; the great god Adäi lived among them. In their paradise tools worked by themselves while people just looked after them. But one day the humans got drunk and forgot to look after their tools. So the tools rebelled, and forever after people had to work hard on Earth.

The Greek poet Hesiod said that the four mortal races were created one after another by the gods; of gold, silver, bronze and iron. The first lived in peace and plenty, the second so extravagantly that the god Zeus entombed them to punish them. The bronze people who followed killed one another in wars, and the last people, made of iron, knew only tiredness and trouble.

In contrast, a happy North American legend tells how the coyote took away people's immortality for their own good, believing that otherwise they would eventually become bored by eternal life!

The clumsiness or laziness of the gods could be held responsible for differences between humans. The Chinese goddess Kiu-Kua began to model the first people from fine yellow clay. But this was a time-consuming job which needed careful attention, and she quickly lost patience. She ended up by shaping people roughly out of a thread dipped in mud. The Chinese believed that nobles were descended from the figures of clay, while the ordinary people came from the far more numerous figures of mud.

The golden age

Some people believed that the first people, like gods, did not work and suffered no pain. And they were immortal. Their foolishness or their pride were punished by all the problems of disease, hardship and death, which troubled their descendants.

▷ THE WORLD'S GRAIN STORE ◁

The god Amma created Earth from a handful of clay, which he dried and then threw into space, where it stretched from north to south and from east to west. At first Earth was just a dry desert; then Amma sent down rain to make it fertile. Next he modeled four men and four women from clay and sent them down to Earth to be the ancestors of all people.

After a time Amma called the ancestors back to the Sky. He forbade them to meet one another in case they quarreled. For food, he gave each the seeds of eight food plants including millet, rice, and beans; the smallest seed, digitaria, was so difficult to prepare that the first of the eight ancestors swore that he would never eat it.

At last all the seeds but the tiny digitaria had been used up; The First Ancestor decided to eat his, after all, and because he had broken his oath, he was considered unworthy to stay in the Sky. Sadly he got ready to return to Earth. He remembered the miserable conditions of the people he had left behind there. They lived like ants in tunnels beneath the ground; they had no tools and no fire. Their limbs – like those of the eight ancestors – had no joints; they were like snake's bodies.

Before he left the Sky, the First Ancestor collected together everything he thought might be useful on Earth. He rounded up a male and a female of all the animals which were then unknown there – sheep and hens, goats, cats, dogs, even mice and rats; the larger animals included antelopes, hyenas, lions, monkeys and elephants. He did not forget birds, insects and fish. He chose plants including the baobab and,

of course, the eight food plants. And he decided to take bellows, a hammer and an anvil with him so that he could teach people to make tools with them.

All this would make a heavy and cumbersome load, but the First Ancestor thought of a way to get around that. He built a huge pyramid, with a round base and a flat top. Inside, he made eight compartments where he stored the eight food plants. On the sides he made a number of ledges on which he placed the animals and plants. He fixed an arrow firmly in the center of the top, and wound a strong thread around it. He attached the loose end of the thread to another arrow, which he thrust into the Sky. His last act was to steal a fragment of the Sun from the blacksmiths of the Sky in order to take fire to Earth. Then he launched his amazing edifice down a rainbow; while the thread unwound, he perched on the top to fight off attacks.

When the blacksmiths discovered their loss they were furious, and hurled flaming sticks at the thief. Meanwhile, the pyramid sped faster and faster until it crashed to Earth. The First Ancestor lost his balance and fell, breaking his supple limbs on the hammer and anvil. The breaks healed as useful joints, and at the same time similar joints appeared in the limbs of all the people of Earth. Then the First Ancestor marked out the first field, the first village, and the first forge. He taught people to cultivate their land.

Soon the seven other ancestors joined him, each bringing new skills to make life on Earth easier and more pleasant.

The First Ancestor launched his laden pyramid down the rainbow toward Earth.

THE FISH WITH THE GOLDEN HORN

One sunrise Wise Manu was walking along the banks of the sacred river. He scooped up some water in his hands to sprinkle over his body as he said his morning prayers. By mistake he caught a tiny shimmering fish, its scales as bright as gold. On its head was a strange horn. "What kind of fish can this be?" Manu asked himself, preparing to throw it back. Then he heard a soft voice saying: "O Wise Manu, I beg you not to throw me back into the river! I will only be gobbled up by a larger fish."

"This fish knows my name; it must be a messenger from a god," thought Manu. Carrying the tiny creature carefully in his cupped hands, he hurried home and put it in a large jar of fresh water.

The next morning Manu was woken by loud noises from the jar. He ran over to it to find the

golden fish had grown a hundred times bigger in the night; it filled the jar completely. Manu picked up the jar, ran to a pond nearby, and threw in the fish. The next day the pond had become too small for the fish. So Manu carried it to a lake; before long the fish had grown out of that too. With great difficulty, Manu carried it down to the sea.

By now the fish was immense. Its scales glittered so dazzlingly that Manu had to shade his eyes as he looked at it. But the fish did not swim away. "I can do nothing more for you," called poor Manu. "But please tell me who you are."

"I am the god Vishnu who watches over the world," replied the fish. "I left my heavenly home because Earth will soon be flooded, and all living creatures on it will be drowned unless you do as I say. I took the form of the fish to lead you to the sea. Now I will send you a boat large enough to carry a pair of each of the kinds of animal living on Earth. Collect them together without delay. I will keep my fishy shape so that I can watch over you."

When the world was flooded Vishnu towed Manu and his boat to the mountains where he could wait safely until the storms were over and the flood waters had gone down; and so life on Earth was saved.

During the flood, the fish with the golden horn watched over Manu and his boat.

▷ NOAH'S ARK ◁

Many years had passed since God first made the world. He watched carefully over his creation, and after a time what he saw distressed him deeply. People everywhere were wicked and violent, following their worst instincts.

"How I wish that I had never created people," thought God. "If they go on like this, they will put the whole world in danger." He decided to wipe them off the face of the Earth, and with them all the animals he had created.

This decision made God very sad, for there was just one man whom he knew did not deserve punishment. He was called Noah, and for more than fifty years he had been just and good and had always obeyed God. So God called Noah and said:

"I have decided to rid the Earth of all creatures now living on it, for they have been corrupted by people. But I want to save you because you are a good man; and thanks to you life will be reborn if you will do as I ask. Build a boat of wood and reeds and take shelter in it with your wife and your sons and their wives; I am going to drown the Earth in a great flood. Fill the boat with a pair of each kind of animal, and with all the different plants, with which to restock the Earth when I decide that the time has come for the floods to go down again."

Noah did as God asked. He built a huge boat, which he called an ark. It had a large door in the side, and one tiny window high in its roof. When his ark was ready, Noah called the animals. Two by two, they entered the ark as God had ordered. When the animals, provisions to feed them all for a long time, and plants had been loaded, Noah and his family boarded the ark and sealed it up to make it watertight.

Just as he had promised, God sent down torrential rain for forty days and forty nights, until the Earth was completely flooded. All life on Earth was drowned except for Noah and the animals he had saved. For another forty days the ark drifted on the water until God sent a powerful wind which gradually dried out the land.

Seven months after the beginning of the flood, the bottom of the ark scraped on something solid. It had come to rest on the peak of a high mountain. Safe and sound, but very tired, the survivors longed to leave their refuge, but Noah was cautious. "We must make sure that the floods have gone down enough," he said. He opened the one tiny window and sent out a raven, who soon flew back; it had found nowhere to perch above the surface of the water. Then Noah sent out a dove; and again it soon returned.

"Be patient," Noah pleaded. And he waited seven days before sending out another dove. They waited anxiously until evening, when it returned with an olive twig in its beak.

Seven days later Noah sent out the dove again and this time it did not return. Noah knew that it must have found dry land to build its nest. He opened up the ark, and all the animals streamed out. "Be fruitful and multiply," commanded God. Never again will I curse the creatures of the Earth." And to show that he meant his promise, God threw a beautiful rainbow across the sky.

Safe and sound, Noah and his animals rejoiced at the end of the Flood.

▷ MYTHS ABOUT ANIMALS ◁

According to many mythologies, the gods created animals during their early attempts to make perfect living creatures, before they created people. The Maya gods condemned animals to be hunted forever because they were imperfect. However, other stories show animals as valued helpers or advisors of the gods in creating the world. Gods frequently took the shape of animals when they visited Earth, and American Indians told how, long ago, people and animals could change from one form to another as they wished.

Birds

Birds are often shown as companions of the creator gods. Seabirds were particularly useful, as they could move through both sky and ocean. Birds' regular migrations caught the imagination of people, who believed that they were journeying to another world. The people of Alaska believed that their god had taken the form of a raven and flown down to Earth to create its plants. Later he gave people light, against the advice of the fox who preferred to hunt in the dark! Other myths tell how an eagle (in Finland) or a swan (in India) laid the egg which gave birth to the world.

The fish, the crab, and the leech

The people of Micronesia tell how fishes, the children of the deep-sea goddess, built a vast tower on the ocean floor. Eventually it rose above the surface of the ocean

and became the first island. Bengalis thought that the creator sent a turtle and a crab down to the depths of the ocean to find mud with which to build the Earth. But both of them lost the precious materials as they swam up to the surface. Finally they said a leech managed to carry out this vital task successfully. It did so by swallowing the mud so that it was not washed away during the long swim. In Melanesia Earth tremors were said to be caused by a giant crab which lived in the bottom of the ocean.

The chameleon

The Pygmies regarded the chameleon as a sacred animal. Close to the creator god, it was able to climb to the top of the tallest trees. One day the chameleon heard a noise coming from the trunk of a tree; it split the trunk, and a large wave rushed out which flowed over the earth as a number of great rivers. Next the first man and the first woman appeared from the tree. Their eldest child be-

came the ancestor of the Pygmies, and the second the ancestor of the Negroes.

The bear and the dog

A long time ago the god of the sky sent down to Siberia a bear who was none other than his own son. This bear brought people fire, and taught them how to make weapons. He promised never to attack a human, and people regarded him as a god. But one day the bear forgot his promise; and ever since his descendants have been hunted like the other animals.

The dog nearly brought a terrible catastrophe to Africa. It stole fire from a rainbow, and brought it down to Earth on the tip of its tail; but when it landed, the undergrowth caught fire. Fortunately people managed to get the flames under control, and they were able to keep and use the precious gift of fire for themselves.

People have always invented myths and legends to explain things they did not understand. Over many centuries former mysteries have become clear and early explanations have been swept away by proven facts. But there are still many things which we do not know. Scientists tell us what they think happened, but even their ideas are constantly changing as new facts come to light.

The ancient Babylonians recorded their observations of the movements of the stars.

The Universe contains many star groups called galaxies. Our galaxy is spiral-shaped like the one on the right.

One result of this is that you may find two books which give dates that differ by many millions of years for the first life on Earth, for example. Both dates were thought correct when each book was written, but new knowledge or techniques made scientists alter their conclusions.

The Universe

Our knowledge of the Universe has been built up gradually over the centuries from painstakingly recorded observations of the sky at night. The first people, who had no instruments to help them, noticed the positions of the stars. They soon realized that some seemed fixed, and others appeared to move across the sky. They noted down what they saw. There were practical reasons for knowing the positions of the stars at different times of night, and in different seasons. The knowledge helped farmers to make calendars for sowing and harvesting, and guided travelers at night.

Later astronomers – as people who study the stars are known – developed instruments to help them make their observations. The telescope was invented at the beginning of the 17th century. It revealed that the Universe was far bigger than anyone had ever imagined, and that there were many stars which could not be seen with the naked eye. Since then astronomers have developed even bigger and better telescopes which pick up radio waves sent out by the stars; they have given us a great deal more valuable information.

Modern telescopes are housed in huge observatories. Some of them have been built on top of mountains, away from the dust, pollution, and glare of cities which make it harder to see the stars. In 1990 the Hubble telescope was launched into space to send back pictures to Earth so that we have a view of the stars unobscured by the haze of Earth's atmosphere. The results have been disappointing so far.

The "big bang"

Despite all our scientific advances, we still do not know for sure how the Universe came into being. But it seems probable that it was created in a single giant explosion perhaps 20,000 million years ago. This "big bang" shot matter out in all directions, and the Universe has been expanding outward ever since. Astronomers know that galaxies – vast groups of stars – are moving away from one another at enormous speed, and that the farther they go, the faster they travel. So they think that the Universe is getting larger and larger all the time.

The stars

Stars are born from clouds of gas and dust, whirling through space. These clouds condense until nuclear reactions take place in the center, turning hydrogen into helium. Meanwhile the star gives out light and heat.

New stars are being formed all the time, while others are coming to an end. The Sun is a star, about 5,000 million years old; it is probably about half way through its life. Eventually it will use up its hydrogen. As this begins to happen, it will expand and shine even more brightly for a time, and then it will cool and fade out.

Very large stars – much larger than the Sun – may blow up as they die, flinging the outer layers of gas far into space. An exploding star is called a supernova. Astronomers though the ages have seen and recorded these stars, although they did not know what they were describing.

Stars are grouped together in collections known as galaxies. These galaxies move bodily through the Universe. The Sun is one of around 100,000 million stars which make up the galaxy we call the Milky Way.

The constellations

When we look up at the stars from the Earth, some of them seem to be grouped together in recognizable patterns. We know now that this is usually just because they happen to lie in the same direction from the Earth; they are quite unconnected with one another. But since very early times people have given names to these patterns, or constellations, and woven legends around them. Some were thought to be people or animals who had been transformed into stars by the gods.

Each year the Sun's apparent path

The Earth may have developed from a cloud of cosmic dust.

across the sky crosses 12 such constellations. They are known as the constellations of the Zodiac. Astrologers once believed that these constellations had great influence on people's lives. They drew up charts called horoscopes, which showed the position of the constellations of the Zodiac at someone's birth, from which they claimed to be able to gain much greater knowledge of their character and what was likely to happen to them.

The Sun, the Moon and the planets

Our Sun is just one star among many millions. It looks huge to us, and shines far more brightly than anything else in the sky; but this is only because it is our closest star. Some stars shine many times more brightly, but they are so far away that they do not look so bright.

Because the sun gives us light and warmth, many people have worshiped it. The Moon was thought of as similar to the Sun, but not so bright. Nothing could be further from the truth! While the Sun is a huge burning mass of gases, the Moon is small and cold. It gives no light of its own, but simply reflects light from the Sun. It looks as large as the Sun because it is closer to the Earth.

Both Sun and Moon appear to travel

crust cracked, and molten rock or lava gushed out through volcanoes. Around the Earth was a steamy atmosphere, and water condensed from it to form seas, which now cover more than seven-tenths of the Earth's surface. The heat of the Sun turned some of this water into steam; it rose up into the air, cooled, and fell back to Earth as rain.

Molten rock from inside the Earth spews up through a volcano; many legends described volcanoes as the homes of the gods of the underworld.

Over millions of years shifts in the Earth's crust, the heat of the Sun, and the force of seas and rivers, rain and ice have shaped the Earth into its present form.

The creation of life

People have had many different ideas about the first life forms. Creation legends tell how plants, animals and people were formed by the gods, some-times in their present form but some-times developing and changing later to

Egyptian mythology, like many others, portrayed the Sun as a god.

across the sky. For centuries people thought that the Earth was the center of the Universe, and that the Sun, the Moon, and a number of bright "stars" known as planets traveled around Earth. In the 16th century astronomers showed that this was quite wrong; the Earth and planets travel round the Sun. Now we know that the planets are not stars at all;, but a dense mass of gas or solid matter that reflects lights from the Sun as they travel around it. Earth is just another of the Sun's planets. The Moon, in its turn, travels around the Earth; it is known as a satellite. The Sun, its planets, and their satellites together make up the Solar System.

The Earth

At first the Earth was a boiling mass of molten rock, but gradually it cooled down and a hard crust formed over it. The heat and pressure deep inside the Earth contorted this crust, forming mountains and valleys. Sometimes the

The Bible tells how God created the first people, Adam and Eve, in his own image. This painting dates from the 16th century.

suit conditions on Earth.

Scientists now think that the development of life on Earth has taken place over an unimaginably long time. As far as we know, the first living things on Earth were very tiny cells that floated in the seas about 3,500 million years ago. Plants developed long before animals; the first animals we know of were jellyfish and worms which appeared about 680 million years ago. Very gradually, over millions of years, more complicated plants and animals developed, and some of them moved from the sea to live on land.

Ever since the earliest times plants and animals have changed their forms and become adapted to the places in which they lived. For about 140 million years giant dinosaurs were the dominant creatures on Earth. We know a great deal about them from the fossilized bones left behind. But these vast creatures seem just as strange and improbable as any legendary monsters!

The creation of people

In the middle of the 19th century an English biologist called Charles Darwin put forward a theory which startled and shocked many people. He said that the animals gradually changed and evolved over time; and he said that humans too had evolved, sharing a common ancestor with apes and monkeys. Darwin's theory particularly

Noah sends out a dove to see if the flood has subsided. Archeologists have discovered that there was a terrible flood in the Near East in early times; so legend proves to be founded on fact.

Charles Darwin published his theory of evolution in the late 19th century. Many people were deeply shocked by it.

upset religious people, who believed that God had created all living creatures and that he had specially created humans in his own image. Some people still strongly disagree with Darwin's ideas.

Today scientists agree that our ancestors were ape-like creatures. Over millions of years their descendants came to look more and more like modern people. They stood and walked upright, and around 2 million years ago they learned to use tools. Some 1,500,000 million years ago they began to use fire for cooking and for warming themselves. Modern people first appeared about 40,000 years ago. But humans only learned how to write about 5,500 years ago, so we have no written records of earlier times.

We learn about early life on Earth from fossils – plants and animals that have been turned into stone over many thousands of years. These fossils have usually been buried under layers of rock or mud. Then movements of the Earth's crust have heaved them up to the surface. For a long time people did not realize what fossils were. Now scientists study them and the rocks in which they are found in the most minute detail. Highly skilled techniques such as carbon dating help to tell us how old they are. All the time, our knowledge of Earth's past is increasing.

INDEX